Dear Yukie

Also by Malcolm McFarlane and published by Ginninderra Press
The Water Cart

Malcolm McFarlane

Dear Yukie

Dear Yukie
ISBN 978 1 76109 222 0
Copyright © text Malcolm McFarlane 2021

First published 2021 by
GINNINDERRA PRESS
PO Box 3461 Port Adelaide 5015
www.ginninderrapress.com.au

To Nori Shimizu (Tokyo), Andy O'Sullivan (Fairfax),
Norio Asakura (Akita), Masayuki Sato (Akita),
Dr Chris Sarra (Brisbane) and Eri Inoue (Tanagura)
for your friendship and all that you have taught me

Dear Yukie
I write to you with sadness
news of our friend Arthur
passed away
funeral tomorrow
many days of sadness
just wanted to let you know

Arthur spoke of you often
quite an impression you made
even coaxed a word from me
about you
bijin
his first Japanese word
a beauty he too considered you

bijin indeed
hope you don't mind me saying so
writing to you now
feels good to write
feels like our conversations
so loved by me
our long rambling conversations

Harry's sick with sadness too
sorry about Arthur
glad he was to know I'm writing to you
passes on his regards
you and Hiroyuki both
me too of course
please give my best to your brother

crazy how time passes
months ago now already
you both here
us all here
Arthur with Harry and me
showing you Leopardwood
the vastness and the carvings

that night at Tilpa pub
then farewells at Broken Hill
don't mind admitting how hard that was
airport farewells
so happy to see you here
then suddenly gone
no idea when we'll meet again

Arthur was sick for a while
no one knew
not even he I don't reckon
I did sometimes wonder though
some days he just looked crook
complained of a sore back
but even that only once or twice

knowing about his drinking
attempts to stop
smoking too
made sense he may not be well
but no
in the end
none of that killed him

must have died during the night
cold by the time we found him
snuggled up in his little tent
so awful
so very sad
such an interesting man
imperfections like us all

puzzle I could never solve
Arthur
never work it out now
never will understand him
then again
we can say that about many
ourselves included I suppose

nice though the thought of that *bijin* here
memories of him
with you
your brief visit out here
desolate and vast you called it
though you loved it also
I could tell

you are always truthful
seems to me
remember once saying so
you laughing
only truthful in English you said
harder to deceive
beyond the mother tongue

just the same
I admire honesty
in you and anyone
makes me want to be the same
would always like to be honest with you
to myself of course also
increasingly

so if you don't mind
I'll keep writing to you like this
old-fashioned I know
hardly anyone sends letters now
not by mail anyway
but while we still can let's
at least until we meet again

encourages honesty too
perhaps
at least it does for me
don't think that I could put a lie on the page
writing something down
becomes a kind of promise somehow
in any language

a kind of sense-making too
don't you think
helps me anyway
something about the process
pen in hand
makes me clarify whatever thoughts
perhaps make a bit more sense of the world

please tell me though
when I don't make sense
your English is very good
I don't mean that
it's just that I can be vague sometimes
in thought and deed
so be your honest self please

hope too
you don't mind it like this
my almost verse
not trying to write poems
just feel that this is the best way for me
these short bursts of ideas
putting whatever down without thinking

been writing notes like this for years
just to myself until now
nice to be able to share
flows more honest this way somehow
at least for me it seems
and I could only ever be honest with you
sharing my sense-making of the world

could be a few letters too
one a week perhaps
no need to reply every time
I know how busy you are
from me though once a week
I'll want to write to you every day
but shall restrict it to weekends

plenty of opportunities to be vague
show my indecisive self
hopefully not
hopefully more interesting for you than that
little updates on my life over here
so different to your own
my vast and desolate world

since Arthur's passing
there is a fair bit I should say
or there will hopefully be
lots to report each week
given his recent generosity
his gifts to Harry and I
what he's done I'll try to describe

Arthur as you know
not so long ago
became a very wealthy man
buying Leopardwood
then Kirinya across the river here
my home since a child until late teens
Arthur took the chance to buy that too

estranged from his family for years
grog mostly I think the reason
and his wife earlier died
Arthur has left me the place
Kirinya
plus some money besides
my family home returned to me

Harry of course receiving Leopardwood
ecstatic at the news was he too
the ancient carvings of course
his main concern
now secure
back in the hands of his people
Paarkintji

not sure every letter will contain such big news
but of course I wanted you to know
so sad to lose Arthur
we all are still
so sudden it seemed too
no farewells
no time

sad as it is
such opportunities he's left us
as Harry said the other day
he's left us a different future
something very special
both a gift
and a challenge

remember that afternoon here
Harry showing you around Leopardwood
the amazing carvings of course
but also that piano
a piano the one thing remaining
an otherwise empty home
played by no one for years until you

days later
on the phone
Arthur still raving happy
I could sense his beaming smile
even over the phone
couldn't believe you could create such a sound
music from such a dusty old thing

Chopin he kept saying
she brought Chopin to Leopardwood
laughing though so ill
very keen he was
delighted we stayed in touch
you and I
actually made me promise

then all too soon he was gone
but so nice it is
that memory
you smiling too
beaming a long time I recall
your smile
as beautiful as the music that filled the air

we are nothing without our memories true
certainly that day
a lovely one
poignant now
with Arthur's passing
and you back in Japan
me still remembering you all here

so with a gift and a challenge
I remember fondly
you here
and my time in Japan
especially so with you
best regards
Callum

Dear Yukie
thank you so much
your letter
a treasure
didn't expect your reply so soon
now here's me
late replying it seems

all my big promises
a letter each week
think of you always
yet only this evening making time
working some long days
fencing and more fencing
tired each night but that's good

now all this talk of a virus
perhaps a new beginning
all this isolation enforced
a new thing for many true
not so for you and me
how long apart now
this pandemic just one more blocker

families the first walls
your father
fine man he may be
unmoved in his disapproval of me
my parents adore you
yet want me here
close to them as they age

though now of course
no one can be close
a letter such a fine simple thing
brings you to me somehow
at least that's how I feel
a message of my simple truths
makes me focus on what I have to say

your letter in return
something to hold
something you touched and sealed
a small parcel of hope
amid what seems despair all around
some leaves of life
for me to treasure

such memories of Japan
especially with you and Hiroyuki
up in Akita amid the snow
that lovely Kawabata street
what a thing to see
even before I met you
accidentally I wandered upon it

a meandering narrow street under snow
a beautiful line of bars
neon crouched in snow
single line of cars
taxi tyres creaking fresh dry snow
late I arrived in the day
winter dark came quickly

feeling my way
found a street of small bars
nestled softly in snow
welcome lights
irasshai the warm greeting
walking into each cosy
dusting off the cold

blues bars
some so American in theme
traditional inns too
famous Akita *sake* served warm
perfect it seemed
increasingly so
with each small cup filled

Zapp caught my eye
some beers and *sake* already consumed
enjoyed more than one welcoming tiny bar
Zapp though a little larger
up some stairs a young crowd
good music
Hiroyuki saw me alone

your kind brother bought me a beer
happily and easily speaking in English
soon welcoming me to his table of friends
the group including his beautiful sister
Yukie
and we seem to have been friends ever since
we three

lucky me
such memories of you there and here
the contrasts of our homes
could they be any greater
seasons and language
my vast shimmering plains
while your cold mountains enclose

reflections come in waves
memories of my months there
treasures always
a perfect contrast perhaps
what I am attempting to do here now
Harry too across the way
saw him briefly today

told him I'd received your letter
happy he seemed too
knowing of the connection still
he'd asked me more than once
had I written to you
checking up on me
understanding the importance of you

I mentioned your particular questions
my apologies
thought that it was all clear with you
Arthur's story I mean
his journey from the street to millionaire
landing out here buying Leopardwood
draining the old reservoir up in the rocky hills

discovering the ancient carvings submerged
apologies though
getting that wrong
your questions in the letter I'll try to answer
it is quite a yarn
so much luck involved
fate perhaps yet good decisions made too

inspiring I reckon
Arthur
winning so much money randomly
especially when he was suffering such despair
yet didn't blow it
grabbed the opportunity
did some wonderful things really

sure he travelled around for a bit
working out what he should do
at least so he said to Harry and me
fair enough too I reckon
living on the street as he was
treasured pregnant wife killed by a car
drowning his sorrows without end

finished up losing work and home
family disowned him
such was his overall state of affairs
then one night he comes across a woman
bashed and left to die in the park
so he helps her
cares for her

months later she returns
a thank you gift
a week or so all paid at a fancy hotel
plus a lottery ticket
never sees her again
tries to
especially after that ticket wins

seven million he said it was
just imagine that eh
you hear about it now and then
someone's big win
then next thing a story of it squandered
or bringing nothing but unhappiness
jealousies

not with Arthur though
he travelled
thankful for that am I too
otherwise he wouldn't have met Hiroyuki
then me in Japan too
Akita brought us all together
your beautiful northern town

I suggested he should come out west
just as travellers swap addresses
not that he had a fixed abode
no home to welcome in return
and I think that worried him
so next thing I know here he is
at Broken Hill then Tilpa pub

Harry liked him straight up
without knowing anything about the money
sensed he was a fella who wanted to do something
lots of nice blokes around
Harry likes to say
trouble is though
there're not doing anything

and there is a lot in this world
bellows Harry
that needs to be done
seems that this fella Arthur
wants to do something
snapping up Leopardwood
belongs here I reckon

then came the carvings
that impressed Harry too
soon as he realised what was there
called us both in
seeking advice from Harry
a Paarkintji man
respect given properly

as Arthur described it
came across them on one of his first days
at least one of his first attempts to do something
do something practical
fix something up on the place
cleaning out the water supply
logical place to start

I'd suggested he wait for some help
offered to help too
big job as it would be
but he couldn't wait
had to get things rolling
always better out here to work with a mate
so far from help you see

but he couldn't wait
and here's me now anyway
working most days alone
hypocrite in that too it seems
I know the feelings he would have had
approaching that old reservoir
in the raised rocky outcrop across the way

hills we call them
yet this must amuse you
just a blip on the vast plain
compared to the mighty mountains up your way
so important though out here
any change like that in the terrain
cloud-catchers my dad calls them

water is everything out here of course
a sacred thing
always has been
everywhere
for Japan too naturally
beautiful clean water revered
you just have a lot more of it seems to me

so many gorgeous shrines and temples
water a feature in all
a centrepiece too for many gardens I saw
landscaped pools
or water flowing
the sound of clear water purling
purifying upon entering a temple

up in those Leopardwood hills
those cloud catching hills
some natural pools
some stone cradles
not much bigger than a bath
others wider and deeper
catch the rain when it comes and holds it long

the last water for miles around when it dries
up in those shaded stone pools
those Leopardwood hills
makes sense they were special always
Harry explaining to me
a meeting place for countless generations
for Paarkintji and others besides

makes sense such a special place
life-giving place
attracting animals and birds always
of course it was sacred to all
though sadly too
made sense for an early European settler
to concrete one big section as a deep reservoir

so just imagine then
Arthur
his enthusiasm to get something done
start improving the place
finds the rocky dam choked up with carcasses
rotting goats and roos and whatever else besides
decides it all has to be drained to refresh again

finds a way to smash open old rusty piping
releases the water from the base of the concrete wall
revealing all
a slimy gallery of carvings
images in stone
likely thousands of years old
stinking and slimy but still there

he'd not long met Harry
long enough to trust him though
Arthur with sense and decency enough
contacted Harry and I straight away
emotional we all were
something pretty raw
for Harry especially so

the thing is Yukie
bad as it was
heartless an act as it may have been
crudely concreting and flooding that gallery
filling the need and the greed of the newly arrived
even worse was the thought of what else yet unrevealed
what other crimes still covered in water or sand out here

disturbing too
as Harry noted
thanking Arthur for alerting him
such anxiety about the many things perhaps already found
uncovered by less caring souls
swiftly hidden again to hide the crime and any inconvenience
or worse still sold or used for profit somehow

Arthur was a decent man
though like so many
little knowledge of Aboriginal culture or ways
yet had sense and decency to know
imagine the significance for others of his find
did the right thing
more important than the upending of his own plans

and a special find it has turned out to be
the whole community excited
gradually making their way up here to see
not to mention the universities
quite a stream of academic types
looking impressed
pondering preservation

I have this sense that there is so much more
stuff yet uncovered and as Harry says
stuff covered back over again
such is the great unsaid in Australia
the details of the brutal occupation of the land
many things too of course not tangible things to reveal
deeds perpetrated and swiftly submerged

history so important everywhere
important to learn and retell
crucial to establish the facts
face the shame if it is there
offer apologies if due
learn honestly from whatever ugliness
and move on together in every way

your people too
not so long ago unwelcome colonisers elsewhere
no shortage of atrocities there
or on any land
seems wherever there have been people
conflict a common language
I wonder if it will always be so

honesty and empathy
not such difficult things really
Arthur got it
he came to understand
not from his wealth
though perhaps his great sudden change in circumstance
enabled a recalibration of his place in the world

I think he thought a lot
about the responsibility of opportunity
that's why he didn't blow it I reckon
determined he was
do some good
realised the chance he was given
just a fraction of humanity as lucky as he

not directly anyhow
a single skin cancer
hadn't realised it had flared
taken root in his back
pretty nasty operation
flew to Sydney for it
all too late

Harry and I hadn't heard from him
worried for him
went looking
found him not at home
his home
my old home
instead he was camped down by the river

Uncle Cecil had kept an eye on him
you'd remember Cecil
Harry's uncle
on Kirinya with his team
his young fencing contractors
staying in the old shearers' quarters
not far from where we found Arthur

camped where he chose
down by that old canoe tree
Uncle Cecil knew that he was poorly
checked on him each day
morning and evening
took him food
gratefully accepted but hardly eaten

he'd seen the other side
knew all about life in survival mode
no luxury of forward planning
prioritising what he should do when
no chance of shaping a better future
not when living hand to mouth
each day seeking food and safety only

my travels highlighted this for me
woke me from my stupor
my lucky sleep of being a white male Australian
in itself a kind of lottery win
opportunities aplenty
realised that I can't change the world entirely
but attempting to is the right thing to do

and now with this further windfall
Arthur's so generous gift
sense myself refocussing again
trying to maximise whatever impact I may have
knowing it would be all the richer if you were here
fondly
Callum

Dear Yukie
the season here is a challenge
the season everywhere
the climate everywhere
a challenge increasing it seems
saw footage of your recent typhoons
droughts and fires here worse than ever

easy to despair
don't you think
easy to feel worries unending
especially when you take pause
stop to ponder
in our otherwise crazy busy world
thinking can lead to worries without end

an amazing thing the mind
anxieties from nothing created
then rationality and calm
solutions quelling fears
all phases within the same mind
moments apart
what a thing the human mind

such beauty can be the outcome
or brutality unspeakable
all from the same flesh
our countries examples of both
plus all phases in between
different parts of history
every country may hold the same extremes

bloodshed on every land
along this river right here too
things I'm only beginning to know
especially the first few decades
we Europeans came
shocking even the fragments I have learned
scares me to consider the actual ugly scale

murder and retribution
theft and killings
revenge attacks
every river in the country
like this one
blood on the banks for sure
followed by denial for years

then on this same country can you see
so much simple beauty
a frosty winter morning
clear blue skies
an evening campfire smoke
swirling up to stars unimaginable
stars so close that you feel a part of the sparkling whole

insane that on this same stretch of earth
men who looked like me
perhaps even of a similar age
just decades before
sat huddled somewhere
plotting an attack the next day
revenge for some of their sheep taken

and on these same river banks in the 1860s
not so far upstream from Kirinya
well south of Bourke anyway
an infamous police patrol
chained a young Paarkintji man to a tree
shot him and left him there as a warning
brutality beyond imagining

if he shot a dingo
or a wild dog of any kind
my father would hang the carcass from a tree
sling it across a fence line
if there was one nearby
a warning to other beasts perhaps
perish further mauled any remains stiff dried

I wonder how long that poor man killed
left rotting
at the base of that silent tree
a river redgum more than likely
majestic things that span centuries
witness to amicable fishing parties
floods and times of dry

one mighty tree close in to town
famous as the place for generations
a women's place
the birthing tree
high-raised buttress roots
supporting generations of anxious trembling hands
gripping and pushing new life into the world

adding new life to these banks
babies born
released into sure experienced hands
older women who had been there before
gripping the same life-smoothed roots
for their own babes
generation upon generation

so how can it be
a similar tree
used to chain another of the same clan
such hatred
such an atmosphere of anger existed
within the hearts of men
men who may well have looked like me

and how long I wonder
did the body remain
the crumpled bloodied carcass
the remains of a baby once born amid pain and joy
at the base of that birthing tree
left chained to rot in the heat
at night mauled perhaps by dogs wild

were there loved ones who knew
risked further violence
stealing the remains away
somewhat restore a corpse to dignity
perhaps though
no one came
his family grieving elsewhere unaware

shocking to think
these things actually did occur
and not so many years gone
as you saw with your own eyes
Yukie
the carvings uncovered on Leopardwood
dammed into a reservoir in the 1950s it seems

such callous disregard
and yet from all this ugly history
steps the likes of Harry
a proud man looking forward
and Uncle Cecil
and his wonderful niece
nephews too

though ever calm
don't believe there is not anger in their hearts
hatred at the bloodshed
the dispossession
yet it has not often emerged for me to see
these riverbanks soiled with their ancestors' blood
they stride still with knowledge and pride

such wonderful minds
human minds
not letting darkness overtake the light
a constant battle so it is
and with them I feel I have advisors here
mentors in so many things
from an ugly past true beauty can come

honesty is the first thing though
you and Hiroyuki spoke of this to me too
your own country's ugly decisions
being honest about your past
the importance of admitting the brutality
the stupidity of those years of war
your grandfather and his Peace cigarettes

do you remember introducing me to him
that great *raamen* noodle bar in Akita
a crazy place your brother's favourite
the baseball guy
Koshien
that's right
Koshien the high school baseball tournament

the shop owner
can't recall his name now
drinking often as he worked
espousing the purity of the high school baseball comp
comparing it to the harsh world of pro leagues
I remember his teenage son
not so into baseball

winter it was when I first went there
a hot tea he handed me as a welcome from the cold
though not just tea it seemed
wheat tea
mugi-cha
with a decent slug of *shocchu* rice spirit
a hot toddie my Scottish ancestors would have approved

so much life in that little quirky bar
your brother's favourite he enthused
the owner's nostalgia for a more innocent Japan
the many optimisms of youth
emblazoned on the walls in his own calligraphy hand
proverbs Hiroyuki explained
a cluttered but somehow special place

I sensed though it was not your favourite place
yes it is fun
you said to me
if far from clean
and I could not disagree with you there
in fact the more I looked
the more your summation was true

many times I returned
during my year there
sometimes with Hiroyuki
only once though that first time with you
Akita bijin
that interesting owner said to me
pointing directly at you

everyone laughed when I guessed correctly
including you I recall
though perhaps a little bemused too
me suggesting *bijin* might mean beauty
seemed obvious to me
the shabby funny little cramped noodle bar
accentuating your elegance even more

your grandfather was beaming
lighting another of his cigarettes
unfiltered he would tap out the next from the soft packet
Peace and I remember a dove of perhaps gold
white writing on dark blue
pointing to the word and speaking clearly to me
the only English word he cared to know

I accepted one from him
an occasional smoker then
can still remember the crumbs of tobacco
bitter in my mouth
the strength of the thing as he lit it for me
smiling at our simple communion
Peace

more knowing smiles
as the night unfolded
warm *shocchu* consumed
fervent handshakes as our conversation somehow revealed
both your grandfather and mine
both in Borneo during the war
different sides of a great ignorant divide

no details of the behaviour of either offered
yet there we were
in a quirky earthy bar
in the far north west of Japan
sharing alcohol and Peace cigarettes
recordings of youth baseball on a small TV
and regularly toasting the beauty that was you

nomunication your brother also taught me
the importance in Japan
nomunication
drinking communication
something I feel our countries share
not sure if this is good or bad
not sure

certainly I have done my share
my share of *nomunicating*
both here and in Japan
social creatures that we are
funny that we seem to need some substance
grease the wheels of communication
for good and bad

not so sure you approve always
though I didn't understand the language at the time
your disapproval of Hiroyuki
often clear
funny though he is when he has a few
I do understand
and you could criticise me similarly

it's a fine line
seems to me
between enjoying life
indulging a little
and wasting your days away
better perhaps
to verge on caution

regrets are another way though
don't you think
of wasting your life away
anyone with a thinking mind would have them
the paths not pursued
opportunities not taken
but the only way is forward surely

regrets are a pathway to anxiety I reckon
not pretending I don't have my own
as you well know
but what am I to do
cannot change what is
better to put my energies into today and tomorrow
at least that is my hope anyway

I may not have the finest mind
but ideas and energy seem to be abundant
nothing I can do will undo the history here
bloodshed and ignorance has a long time been here
these banks of the Paarka
Darling River
soaked in sorrow

not a thing that is done can be changed by me
yet as I ponder these solitary evenings
consider this vast country
my not inconsiderable portion of it
it does seem very possible to make a mark
strike a blow for positivity
work respectfully with people and the land

seems so logical to me
and Arthur had made some headway too
talked things through with Harry and me
others too
welcomed Uncle Cecil and his young fencing team
had something of a strategy in the making
restoring some health to the land long term

the river too of course central to it
requiring so many others to think the same
that's a road I'm yet to negotiate
but willing to try
team up with Harry somehow for those battles to come
and native pastures
an obvious choice to my mind

lots to do
Peace lets you do that I guess
impossible otherwise
not sure we appreciate truly
how lucky we are here
seems the real conflict now though
so stupidly with nature

it is like a war
when you think for a moment
at least we should be treating it so
the energies of all
focused on the one thing
a common cause
though any victory unlikely

a civil war really
in conflict with ourselves
all the distress of an internal conflict
divisions common
between friends
within families
opinions becoming emotions

not sure what victory would look like
less catastrophes maybe
temperatures cease to rise
fires less intense
floods and storms decrease
anxieties abate
children smile more often

many generations will now need to do battle
that's another crazy thing
just to prevent total collapse
not just of climate
but societies everywhere
any final victory may never come
yet some small battles won would be sweet

the battle over ignorance
arrogance
entitlement
disconnection from the natural world
selfishness
anger
greed

all human failings exposed
exfoliating in the heat
drowning in the downpours
blown away by the storms
those who wish to fight for their own ends only
their own small piece of the whole
will surely be exposed and consumed

small things will matter
and will feel good to achieve
though only if in line with the whole
only if supporting the greater good
selfishness has to be gone
each battle must involve the whole
supporting the interconnectedness of the world

yes easy to feel overwhelmed
but what else is there to do
simply do and then do some more
even my planning and explaining to you
lifts my mood
fondest regards
Callum

Dear Yukie
I've been considering my small battles
the tangible things I can do
thinking and planning is good
knowing that action is here
steps are being taken
and they are my steps

when discussions here turn to water
as they often do
cotton is the enemy it seems
has been so for some years
sucking so much water with their huge pumps upstream
downstream suffers
the whole river system starved

some have become rich
communities thrived through cotton
but a tough argument now to defend
our increasing dry times
no river flow
cotton has enemies all around it seems
and I've never been a fan

when the first big farms went in
upstream from our place
Kirinya
Dad and Mum were upset straight away
water demands were clear from the start
not right Dad would say in despair
not right the dismal flows

in the civil war on climate
cotton looks like an important hill to win
and a battle I think worthwhile
plenty of resources and strategy required
such is the opposition's size
but we should win through
the common good is on our side

at the pub last night we got talking
yes I'm trying to restrict my visits
just Friday and maybe Saturday nights now
last night Harry and I met in there
spoke a little about the scale of those farms
thousands of acres
laser levelled for crops of cotton

how good would it be
said I to Harry
if we could get hold of one of those places
return the water to the river from their huge catchment dams
then use that bizarrely level ground
not for cotton but something else
plant it out with native cereals

I've been reading some amazing stuff on this
yields are less than wheat
but there are of course varieties native to here
deep-rooted
adapted to the dry
how perfect would that be
thousands of acres of what should be grown here

Harry laughing with pleasure at the thought
we were eating a pub pizza
and he stops and looks at it
inspects it for a moment
then says
how about this for a plan
Paarkintji pizza with a native grain base

wouldn't that be something
and why not
need to be large scale though
make it viable
we're up for trialling it on our places
but maybe need an even bigger scale
like those huge cotton blocks

this got us talking about change
how it happens
how you may cleverly win battles in this war
spoke about alternatives
peace offerings I guess
dealing with the perceived enemy
offer something to create behaviour change

take this cotton idea for a start
one way yes would be to somehow buy them out
land and the water rights
but who has the money for that
so why not instead create an alternative path
give them a different road to follow
like this native cereals idea

seems to me if they can make money
have hardly any water needs suddenly
remove the monoculture of cotton
thousands and thousands of acres returned
enabling some form of biodiversity
if it can be profitable and resistant to dry times
why the hell wouldn't they give it a go

seems better than this stinking feud right now
big decisions about water
don't seem to match the election cycles
so making an attractive pathway may work
as long as the river
as long as the land
can be offered some opportunity to breathe

coal's the other of course
rather than just telling them to shut down
all those families and communities impacted
offer them a different road
a role for government in there for sure
can't tell me there are no jobs in other power sources
solar and other renewables have to be a path to change

anyhow
all good blurting about what others should do
perhaps I should let you know my plans
based on stuff I've read and discussed out here
plus of course what Arthur began
he was stepping in the right direction
all that fencing work begun

so all that will continue
Uncle Cecil and his team
probably years of fencing ahead really
a good small team like that
and we'll think it through
create as many logical paddocks as we can
grazing it and locking it off is the thing

my understanding is still evolving too
I've changed from wanting no cattle or sheep at all
to taking a kind of middle way
from what I've been reading
seems they have a role to play
regenerating land
how to manage stock is the key

seems that if you intensively graze
one section at a time
let them disturb the soil for a short time
in a good way
all the while fertilising it as they go
then move them on
let that patch rest and recover is the way

if we have a bit of moisture all the better
though there's no way to count on that out here
but even without
let the bugs and things do their work
break everything down
draw the nutrients back into the soil
should be better than it was

so my hope will be that before too many years go by
there'll be a rotation across the whole place
these introduced ruminants will help improve the soil
not on any one patch long enough to destroy
but there long enough to add plenty of good stuff
roos and other natives of course too
and all the while expelling pigs goats and dogs

no small thing to tackle to be sure
but I have to say to you Yukie
just plotting it out roughly to you now
rolling it over in my head as I always do
talking different things through with Harry too
any way I think on it
excites me like nothing else

I know this is only one patch of the world
seventy-five thousands acres though it may be
nothing in the whole scheme of things
just a spot within the whole state
let alone the rest of the world
but it's doing the right thing that's the thing
redressing at least some harm

such a thing Arthur has done
leaving this land to Harry and I
miss him a lot
but so grateful for this chance he's offered
the trust he showed
and want to do him proud
want to work hard in the right ways

my mum and dad too
want to see their joy continue
each time they come back to the place
we don't agree on all things
my ideas about native pastures especially
but that's okay
our disagreements help clarify my thinking

this one block on the Paarka may not change the world
but it's the right thing to do
absolutely
and good things lead to good things
examples for others
just as I'm learning from others having a go
close by too there are mentors aplenty

just upstream from Tilpa
an important place
famous old property
Kallara
they've been an organic block for years
a huge shed full of bails of gorgeous hay
mixed native pastures supplying farms in the east

no laser levelling on that place
yet there you have it
country cared for
not overstocked and flogged
excess pastures in a decent season
and income created
people employed

lots of work of course
not many sleep ins out here
not if you're having a go
but that's good isn't it
work is the thing
good work makes you feel good
it's hard workers I've always respected

do you remember telling me that Buddhist proverb
I was chopping up some wood for the fire
that night we all camped over on Leopardwood
before enlightenment
chop wood carry water
after enlightenment
chop wood carry water

such a good thing
so apt for out here too
I do love to chop wood at times
and most years there'll be cause to carry water
for stock and people both
it does help though doesn't it
when the work is a thing enjoyed

was the word *samu*
that's what I think you told me
your Japanese word for mindfulness in work
another Buddhist thing I presume
I'm not pretending that's me every day
but I do understand the intent
not a concept totally foreign to me

seems that many people work so that they can stop
whether it's working until the weekend
or trying to retire as soon as possible
whatever that means
doing whatever will bring the most money
not caring about the worth of the work
just the money in return

I've been guilty of it too at times
lots of jobs I haven't done for any pleasure
the paycheque was the thing
no learning or intrinsic pleasure involved
but how much better it is
would it be for all
if the work was the thing that mattered

even for your own state of mind
surely better to do things you enjoy
may not be changing the world
may not be about the environment
nor regenerating land like I'm hoping to
but better still if it does
at least that's my ideal

doing something of worth
hopefully everyone's ideal
and if we are honest
about this being a time of war
the thing of worth
should probably not be a personal thing
but efforts that assist the common cause

complex though it is
makes sense to me
just so grateful for my opportunity
Arthur's gift to let me do things out here
unforgivable if I don't give it a proper go
progress will be slow
but the work is the reward

plenty to do
plenty of space here too
if any Akita *bijin* would care to join me
know it's a lot to ask
just want you to know you are always welcome
fond regards
Callum

Dear Yukie
thank you so much for your letter
received yesterday
interesting that you know of the fires
some terrible fires here
all over the east
making news elsewhere it seems

I have no TV and my internet is often slow
but have seen plenty of images in at the pub
madness the extent of the thing
and the intensity of the blazes
years of dry
temperatures rising
summers lengthening

homes lost
people dead from heat smoke or flames
pastures gone
forests devastated
stock lost or wandering in a daze
then the wildlife
a billion creatures gone they say

finally rains came
too much at once
often the case in this fragile country here
so welcome but problems too
ash consuming waterways
big fish kills
problems cascade

out here in the western districts
no sign of floods nor flames
just the slow burn of the long dry
the earth is resting
so Harry said his old Aunty would say
a drought gives the land time to rest
certainly a positive view of these hard years out here

not that it's stopped Uncle Cecil and his team
they pull up early when the heat is on
but steady progress still made
working on some goat enclosures
done some traps for wild pigs too
they've dropped off a bit in the dry
too many though even so

one feral animal is one too many for me
such damage they can do to this fragile soil
digging around as they do
you'd think someone had dragged through with an old chisel plough
there's a market for pigs too though
Europe it seems
getting some shooters in again soon I'm planning

such a hard thing
getting rid of them entirely
my initial idea
Arthur's too early on
put some kind of barrier right around
fence out pigs goats and dogs entirely
some kind of expensive perimeter fence that would have been

not practical though really
given the many kilometres involved
and not just the initial expense either
seems we'd be excluding roos and other native creatures too
and that didn't make sense
so instead we'll complete a simple boundary fence line
plus build these internal traps as we've started

not sure how much any of this will fascinate you
but it does intrigue me
the clever designs of these things
small enclosures designed to ensnare
built near whatever water remains in our several earth dams
water is the attraction
then the trap closes behind

pig traps are a fairly simple thing
easy to move around too
once there's some obvious activity somewhere
we can put one up pretty quickly
just a circle of metal reinforcement mesh
a few metres across
held up by stiff metal star posts

the gate is just an overlap of the circle
the pigs squeeze in through
attracted by some kind of bait or grain
they can squeeze between the two overlapped sections of mesh
then it springs closed behind
couldn't be simpler
though it has to be strong enough then to hold them

and strength is a thing a wild pig does not lack
especially of course the big boars
tusks and all not a pretty sight
but so far we've only had one fail
they hooked up underneath the mesh
made a weak point and were gone
so that taught me a thing or two

but there is a market all right
we've been shooting the big ones straight away
straight into the chiller
and a buyer comes through when we have a few
Germany and France he reckons they end up
seems the wild meat there is now rare
good money for it too

the young ones caught we've started to keep and fatten
dad thought I was mad
putting good grain into a feral thing
but then he saw money coming back in
not a lot but it is there
direct cash for the carcass cleaned
cash from the chiller operator to Uncle Cecil's young fellas

that caused a few smiles
cash in hand
and seems to me there is a lot of money to be made there
pretty hard grisly work
but just the same
it's a market ready made
and such a good thing for the land to see them gone

not that there seems to be an end to them
even with this long dry
too often I see some
or at least the damage they've caused
millions across the whole country they say
just off this place and Leopardwood across the river
we could probably shoot and trap all year round

we have to go down to Wilcannia though
that's the nearest chiller yard
do you remember
you or Hiroyuki asked about the line of refrigeration vans
looked strange just sitting in a vacant lot
those same chillers we've now started to use
have a mind to get at least one up here though too

depends on the operator
would have to be worth their while to come up here
the couple of hours up this way
but you never know
might be a whole circuit for them
collecting the carcasses of a pest
creating delicacies for folks on the other side of the world

funny world when you think on it
a huge problem could be a good thing
solid income stream for some locals here
a huge help in regenerating the land
and food appreciated by palates elsewhere
just needs a bit more coordinating maybe
but logic doesn't seem to always match the present world

speaking to some hunters
in at the pub the other night
rolling these ideas around
they are sure there'll be pigs for years
but professional hunters are the thing
I knew they had to be licensed and all
but the costs seem to not favour them

seems they need to pay hundreds each year
just for a licence to shoot
now they should be accredited sure
have to be crack shots after all
but why so expensive to do a good thing
we need people to want to do it
why some nonsense barrier to do an essential thing

I reckon I might pursue this
perhaps getting my own licence would be the thing
roo shooting too seems not a very profitable thing
madness it seems
forgetting all the emotion of shooting kangaroos
they are one of the best meats for you
and of course native here

apart from the land use debate
cattle and sheep on this marginal land
the methane and water debate is won by roos hands down
so my ideal is this
go hard with pigs and goats
an industry in their meat until their numbers get cut right down
down to zero would be one potential end game

all the while improving country as I explained before
large mobs intensively grazed
moved on so the country rests properly
encourages all the varieties of native herbage to return
cattle and sheep
ruminants belching methane though they be
perhaps a means to a worthy end

then some day
one happier time
when this part of the world is free of introduced ferals
the country somewhat fertile once again
encourage the native meat industry
let it flourish somehow
better for human health and the whole ecosystem

makes total sense to me
that industry too would require some incentives
investments beyond my means
wouldn't be anything like the millions though surely
billions perhaps pumped into that cotton game
channelled into that and many other enterprises
unsustainable industrial agriculture all

just thinking the other day
ironic I guess my situation now
in the same way with Arthur
his money free to choose his own way
much as I was fond of him
am still and he's sadly missed
it did exasperate some including me his lucky wealth

never met anyone on the land with money at hand
they exist I know
but never in my orbit
mum and dad and all they knew
all their energy and drive
sold up with not much to spare
sold before the bank told them to

not used to it still
trying to go real slow
spending not much at all
more than anything
want to think and plan
conscious too
of what others think

makes sense Harry and I speak so often
two pillars to the same bridge
so Harry said the other day
and I like that image too
different journeys but the same predicament
same opportunity
regenerate everything on our opposing pieces of land

apologies for rambling on so
it does help me though
makes me clear out my too many thoughts
like speaking to you
as if you were here
how I wish you were here
Callum

Dear Yukie
how swiftly things can change
seems like only days ago
first news I saw
a possible health crisis
media full of this virus news
how quickly the world seems to have changed

pandemic now declared
the stuff of movies surely
but so real
even out here
funny Harry said just yesterday
he called to check in with his cranky neighbour
as he always says

he wondered how much more isolated we could be
me on seventy-five thousand acres alone
him across the river on Leopardwood bigger still
just Uncle Cyril and his young team
a few kilometres away towards the river
though they may yet want to head back
down to their Wilcannia homes

so how are you handling it Callum
Harry asks very seriously
managing the two-metre social distancing OK over there
then all I hear is his deep chuckle laugh
isolating okay are ye before he continues
serious again
worried for his family and community

so many houses overcrowded
full up despite all this land and clear wide skies
diabetes and smoking besides
lots of health issues in the best of times
a new virus could burn through real quick
a fire in tall dry grass
hot wind roaring it on

these letters even more important for me
before any pandemic they already were
my little lifeline to you
a clearing house of ideas
and my only remaining delightful connection
to you
and to Japan

more important I guess now
borders closing everywhere
talk of international travel gone
travel something we can't consider
so many freedoms
taken for granted
gone

saddens me no end
yet I so want to be hopeful
heard a fabulous quotation the other day
Pablo Casals
you may know him with your musical education
but I was ignorant until hearing this
these strong words

the situation is hopeless
we must take the next step
so said Pablo Casals
the cellist who I learned we need to thank
without whom modern ears may not know Bach
or at least the cello suites
quite a man it seems

his *Song of the Birds*
a breathtaking thing I came across
traditional music from his native Spain
his tears of reverence can be imagined
across the aching resonance of the strings
just a few days ago
I knew nothing of him

I wonder about the so many lives
inspiration
yet unknown to me
examples of hardships overcome
seems pretty relevant now
suddenly the situation for many may seem hopeless
yet we must take the next step

I think too about the arc of his life
Casals I mean
well into his nineties when he died
a life spanning from the 1870s to the 1970s
such change he would have seen
all the while developing his craft
with a reputation as a humanitarian

I've been collecting quotes for a while now
unintentionally formed something of a collection
jotting them down in a little notebook
one I bought in Akita actually
lovely fine paper and a creamy cloth cover
you make such things so well in Japan
paper not purely a utilitarian thing

not sure if it was Martin Luther King
or President Obama quoting him
I heard somewhere some time ago
Casals's long life reminded me
something like
the arc of history is long
but it bends towards justice

possible don't you think
reassuring
given these times we are in
some comfort to consider much longer term
things may work out yet
looking not at our boots but the far horizon
there may be some justice yet

heaven knows it may take a while anyway
address all the ills we've foisted on the earth
yet think about the length of a life
especially if long like Casals
the potential
the impact you may have
endless if there is a sense of focus

my father was laughing at me the other day
spent a few days over here
helping fix a roof section of the wool shed
it was hot and hard and I don't like heights anyway
I made some comment about being too old
too old to be up there all day
should have paid someone to come in

well did he have a crack at me over that
easy come easy go all this money
you young fellas
he went on
and fair enough too
but then he started to talk about age
enjoying ageing

mentioned old Stan
a lifelong friend of his father's
passed away just a few weeks before
a very significant man
last of all those old ones
my grandfather gone years ago now
just the way of things my father pondered

then he spoke about this old friend some more
recalling a time when he worked with his father
by no means a young man at the time
but full of life
about the same age my own father is now
and dad a young man still
approaching sixty

so what struck him
my father I mean
was how that period was so long ago
though well into his middle age
look at all the things Stan had done since
bought and sold a couple more places
always working hard

it's not just that you are young and then old
muddling along
you actually can do a lot
inhabit a long arc
maybe not always historic
but hopefully of worth
years well lived

focus is important too
don't you think
dad didn't mention this
but I've thought a lot about it since
all good to have time
opportunities
but you have to focus on getting things done

I mean look at me here
gifted this amazing place
this opportunity
improve at least one little part of the world
but nothing will happen
nothing good will emerge
if I have no focus

and I'm still working on it may I say
hate the feeling of time wasted
that I may have idled hours away
pondering
or worse still
just yarning and drinking and carrying on
time squandered

though it's no good rushing either
doing things right is important after all
I don't like panic
but now more than ever
feel time is ticking away
not just for my life
but humanity it seems

whether this pandemic
or the whole climate change thing
a bloke could stress out on any given day
worry about you over there
though at least you are not in huge city crowds
miss you so
love Callum

Dear Yukie
this morning the coldest for the year
not the first frost
bitterly cold though until the sun emerged just now
I picked some mandarins
mum always said you have to wait until the first few frosts
reminded me of persimmons and you

do you remember one late winter day
hadn't known you that long
with Hiroyuki we walked to the top of Senshuu park
across the moat up through the old castle site
looking down across the river
a dusting of snow
cold and grey

a flash of colour caught my eye
beneath a slightly distant eave
a simple older house
hanging from its elegant sweeping curved roof beams
persimmons
drying as they hung in strings
the rich deep orange a flash of life somehow

your winter
such a beautiful thing
despite the long cold
the often inconvenience of snow
slush to walk through
ice to slip upon
rarely the perfect creaky lovely powder

watching from my balcony
despite the cold
I'd roll a cigarette
endure frosty air for a few moments
note the comings and goings below
dark and often windy nights
the little shoe shop across the way

remember the sounds of my small apartment
wonder if you do too
two rooms of six tatami
spacious you told me
you Australians do not appreciate space
so wide and open is your own land
two rooms and your own kitchen space plenty enough

the regular automatic door
just below my six tatami room
my apartment on the second floor
every coming and going from the building
known to me with the door's slow whir
didn't notice it after a while
as a family by the railway oblivious to trains

you though made mention
not just the first time you stayed
that quirky little boss of mine
you told me
no doubt happy
less rent to pay
reduced for noise

from that balcony
four seasons did I observe
rolled cigarette red glow
only light from my balcony
sound of bicycle bells and rim brakes below
lonely
but for you

winter when I arrived
such snow
local hotpots delicious shared
the magic warmth of a low table
spring suddenly
blossoms everywhere it seemed
your seasons so distinctly change

summer humidity
that magnificent festival
Kanto
the whole city
your wonderful small city
a coming together for all
another summer of life celebrated

won't forget those few days
my apartment too
couldn't see it from there
but central enough
could sense the festival excitement
from my little narrow balcony
streets awash with sake and summer beers

huge long bamboo poles metres high
masts of lanterns decorated
candles burning within paper globes
held aloft on a palm or even a chin of the brave
fifty or sixty kilos each Hiroyuki explained
displays of balance and strength
giant heads of rice giving thanks for harvest

then autumn came
distant mountains ablaze
alight with the colours of dying leaves
Tazawa Lake
Hiroyuki and your friends
that hot spa we had to walk to
deep in the mountains

no cars allowed
worth every step along that well-trodden path
open air baths
centuries old
no electricity
piping hot
you declared me a lobster when I finally emerged

I love my veranda here too
something though of a different view
as you said while here
it is possible
in many places
even from a slight rise or crest or raised veranda
to see the earth's curve

and so I sit here on Kirinya
with such sweet memories
the loveliest of course containing you
remembering that narrow balcony
electric automatic door
busy street below
bicycle bells

a door or two down and across from me
very traditional home
stone and timber entrance way
women coming and going in kimono
a teacher of tea I think you said
women skate as they walk with purpose
on pristine linen feet

such memories of that one place
my little balcony
my little window onto a fascinating world
been thinking about our trip too
that summer
down to Nagasaki
your university friend's wedding

that was something
deciding with the help of beers as I recall
during Kanto
hitch our way in your safe country
or ride local trains
try to travel slowly in your fast country
for the fun of it

your friend's grandfather's studio
set high among the winding climbing streets
your bay city
Japan's San Francisco you told me
Nagasaki
the hills and many harbour bays
city of nostalgia and romance

arriving late afternoon
festival underway
lanterns held and carried
floats large and small
boats to carry the souls of the dead
departing from every street it seemed
heading for the harbour to be launched

souls to return
tributaries of flickering light becoming streams
offerings held aloft
destination reached
a night harbour calm
such tradition
such beauty

impossible to imagine the carnage
amid so much life and grace
same city
different time
such a different time
decades before
so much destruction before

and the old man had lived it
that elegant definite man
our grandfather for the night
an artist of renown you explained
we slept on his studio floor
a close humid night
following a long meal and rememberings aplenty

a teenage soldier on watch
that ageing man retold
aware of the blast
from some many miles away
the cloud the glow
the fear and mystery
a mighty unknown thing

and there he was
before us
explaining the devastation yet again
sharing something awful
so that it be known as real
informing the young before him
plus this fellow from another land

such an effort
must have been
rebuilding
creating a city again
his life too
just one of millions
built a life of meaning upon scorched land

that summer
a month or more of hot weekends
every Sunday we drove
swimming at the beach
you learning to body surf
long lunches at your favourite café
together

so happy you were
more holidays than you'd ever taken
delighted the hospital let you go
the days for Nagasaki especially
guess you are busy now though
nurses are heroes everywhere
and rightly so

worry for you
this virus a thing still so unknown
hope you and Hiroyuki are well
troubling times
guess no Kanto nor Obon for now
no social distancing there
annual bondings for your society

wonder if that's happened before
even in times of war
were these ancient rituals
hundreds or thousands of years constant
ever abruptly ceased before
thinking of you in these times of change
Callum

Dear Yukie
thank you for the Peace cigarettes
don't want to smoke them as you know
but at the pub yesterday
went in to pick up the mail
met Harry and Uncle Cecil
old Cecil of course lit one with me

the story of your grandfather he enjoyed
liked the cigarette too
even stronger than his tobacco he rolls so thin
I gave him a couple more
happily accepted
deposited safely
snug within his worn leather tobacco pouch

then driving home in the late afternoon
I stopped again at a favourite spot of mine
just a simple little turn in the track
not far from home
a nice little group of mulga trees
a small rivulet depression
like many spots in the dry

something simple and picturesque somehow
stopped there before
not totally sure why
anyhow I lit a Peace cigarette
sat down on the soft dry soil
in the barely shade
and it was exactly the right thing to do

thought of your grandfather
his stooped back
sparkling eyes
repeating the word in that crazy little *raamen* bar
Peace
Peace
smoked it right down to my fingers

no filter of course
the heat at the end on fingers
can still feel the burn in my throat
bitter tobacco buzz for a time
another terrible thing I try not to enjoy
please thank your grandfather again for me
for both the cigarettes and those honest memories

remember too
Cafe Rondo
that cold Akita afternoon I met you there
your fluffy cream jumper
that café within an old warehouse
such an old building with two foot thick walls
you loved the jazz they always played

not sure if you know
it became a bit of a place for me
a place of solitude
never many there
loved the building
resonated history
such a solid certain thing

cream plastered walls
sweeping roofline
a great sound of course also
a warehouse for centuries
protecting grain and barrels of salted food
safe through long winters and summer rains
repurposed to echo with timeless jazz

over on Leopardwood
thought of that warehouse too
the old homestead there made from stone
this lovely blond sandstone from here
Wilcannia sandstone it's come to be known
a small structure of blocks roughly hewn
feet thick and still standing firm

perhaps you remember it
and next time
when you are next here
let's see how jazz sounds in there
next time you are here
Harry wants to restore the piano too
just for you

we could move it
into the old stone house
see how it sounds
what a moment that would be
can see Harry beaming now
my love
Callum

Dear Yukie
so many things small things
trigger memories of you
this isolation perhaps accentuating
somehow more aware
more appreciative
longing for closer times

just this morning
made a pot of tea
nothing special in that
my morning ritual
an early cup of black tea
spoonful of honey a morning treat
a cold morning

warmed my hands around the mug
letting the globule of honey dissolve
made the same for you
both there and here
you liked it too I could see
warming my hands was what ushered nostalgia
another emotive memory wave

winter approached again
remember one morning
one Saturday it would have been
heading to my weekly class at Yokote
that lovely little town
further south and into the mountains
a feeling of real snow country

had to change trains along the way
this morning I sensed the sharp cold returning
bought two coffees
hot cans from a vending machine
stuffed one in each pocket of my long winter coat
hand warmers until the train arrived
hot strong and sweet shots of coffee

felt a sadness sweep over me
not just winter approaching
that melancholy that can accompany cold
my time there also disappearing
a return ticket with a date looming
work had been offered back home
decisions had to be made

your father had shared his views
very happy for me to return
unaccompanied
no question of his daughter departing
and I could see the torment in you
hated to see you sad
couldn't stop you being sad

our compromise
me to return for a time
you to visit out here
and thus far all to plan
though the heartache still there
still I feel sadness looming
still clutching those warm coffee cans

of all the lovely times together here
it wasn't the trip to Sydney
that great concert
lush hotel
though all that was properly grand
it was that evening you woke me
out here

I'd so looked forward to your visit
then that hard few days unexpected
just after you'd arrived
Uncle Cecil sick and me worried for him
helping his young team
finish the fence line
a section he wanted to complete

I'd fallen asleep as you showered
sleeping deeply
so physically tired
waking in a haze of perfume
a cornucopia of perfumes as you slipped in beside me
sensing you there
holding me

close to me
just you and me in this small room
within this simple timber house
amid the vastness of these acres
totally alone
totally together
this room

so empty without you here
yet I shall never forget that moment
first awaking
realising you there
with me
cupping my face in your hands
to kiss me

I drew you closer
that is all
and that is everything
that is all
in this same room
my love
Callum

Dear Yukie
may I share with you a new word
I know you enjoy learning new words
whether English or Japanese
murmuration
a murmuration of birds
Harry explained today

we were on our bikes
motorbikes
quite a way out
at the last earth dam before my northern boundary
stopped near a section of mallee
low bush all around
startling a huge wave of tiny birds

just cut the bike engines
that lovely instant silence
a motor ceasing amid the otherwise silent air
air immediately exploding
Harry laughing at me
jumping as I did in surprise
scared by a mass of tiny fragile birds

quite the murmuration
Harry declared
watching them form into a cloud
pivot as one
a current of the air
rise and swoop and switch again
then settle finally again elsewhere

at least one good thing
we agreed
one healthy sign for this block here
Harry's Leopardwood too
land flogged as it was both sides of the Paarka
too much stock for years
at least it had not been ripped and cleared

lots of scrub still for some kind of finch
too swift for me to tell exactly
quite a sight
so many as one
and a fine thing too
that new word
murmuration

wonder what that is in Japanese
nice how words cannot always translate
what was it you told me
at Eiheiji
do you remember
the resonant after-sound of the temple bell
yoin

such a brief word in your language
takes some explaining in mine
that was some place too
Eiheiji Temple
so glad you took me there
even the journey
those local trains hugging the rugged coastline

1200 and something
was that right
when the temple first established I mean
more than eight hundred years
eight hundred years people have gathered there
meditating
creating those gorgeous buildings among the trees

remote it must have been
hundreds of years ago
an easy trip for us from Fukui city I recall
but back then
when the first whatever small temple made
a long walk to seclusion it must have been
creating that place of contemplation

Broken Hill to here
now just a few hours on bitumen and dust
a major expedition on horse and dray
back in the day
the world was slower
life at a different pace
a different energy

such avenues of ancient trees
that's the Eiheiji I recall
could sense what you loved there
those sweeping eaves
structures large and small
an uncommon beauty
architecture that seemed to enhance its landscape

so elegantly did it emerge
nestled among mountains
as if always there
stone
fibre and wood
masterfully created
beautifully maintained

samu
another word you taught me
when I mentioned the work involved
must take a lot of work said I
not just building this complex of beauty
everything no doubt done by hand
but also keeping it so

samu if I recall correctly
you explained
mindfulness in labour
even sweeping the stone paths
shovelling the snow
preparing meals
a kind of working meditation

perhaps why such a special place
work performed with *samu*
such history
yet those same rituals still
the days turn
awake to the same resonant bell
despite the very different surrounding world

a lovely thought
Eiheiji
a constant of calm
no doubt today exactly as we were there
stone paths swept
despite everything happening
a world in turmoil

Harry taught me another word
don't often sense his anxiety
now though even he
a usual picture of strength and calm
touches more regularly
on his fears
the many challenges to society

mentioned a thing special to him
a process for people coming together
said a bloke from further north
a western Queensland word
described it as *Engoori*
a coming together after conflict
a traditional way

don't know an English word for it
but as Harry explained
gets all sides listening
being honest
honour the past
envision the future
action the present

so I told Harry
he's got a job to do I reckon
get himself over there
the United Nations
get all those fellas in a circle
put them around a camp fire
lead them through *Engoori*

Harry laughed of course
worries me though
seems we need something special like that
someone to step in
something has to change
stop us heading for these cliffs together
inequities and pandemics and climate change

a bit to consider you could say
I've been reading more and more
trying to make sense of it all
though a task impossible perhaps
one thing I'm finally tackling
a history of philosophy I've had for a while
fascinating I have to say

Harry now calls me Plato of course
Plato the philosopher farmer
so he says
any chance he finds
I just have to mention something
off he goes
yes Plato

think it through now Plato
and if there's a problem of any kind
even the slightest hesitation from me
what would Plato do
what would that old fella do
says Harry
in a situation like this

incredible though
as I see
little that I know perhaps
but as I figure it
we are all seeking the same
and always have
same quest for health and happiness

and not a few formed the view
simple life
close to nature
humble in all things
the path advised
Buddhism
many indigenous people's ways

the Stoics and all that there
Islam too
Christianity has a few question marks
seems to me
wiped out so much
so much of the thinking that went before
that rewriting of history troubles me

history here
so much to clarify here
so much to reveal in this country yet
more and more it troubles me
those Leopardwood carvings
think on that
one thing among many yet to reveal

just think of the generations all gone
here on Paarkintji land
tens of thousands of years
hardship and joy
death and new life
my Scottish ancestors too
struggles but different battles they endured

you in Japan
that fantastic lineage
suffering and beauty
austere times and plenty
our struggles have always been the same
at their heart
no matter when and where

safety
shelter
health
sustenance enough
new life
pockets of meaning
connectedness

hope for our children
procreation
passing life on
peace
such a simple idea
wanted by all
seldom found

yet any brief look at history
our differences are on display
battles of greed and jealousy
based on nothing
at the heart of it
fear and more fear
hate and more hate

our commonality is here now
every person on the planet
anyone from any place
same basic worries today
not sure that has happened before
it has always been so
yet not obviously so

when people have rallied
throughout history
it has been for their cause
their particular passions
not such as now
the same outcome desired
same for every soul

never before
seems to me
in our human history
such common cause
this crippling pandemic
not to mention our climate change
our fragile health and that of the world

yet do we all see this
do our leaders see this
sense this opportunity
chance to erase nonsense squabbles
chance to reset our course
our common cause
surely there is no other way

perhaps me out here
rambling alone
guilty as any I suppose
not exactly taking the lead
no lawmaker have I become
living distant and isolated
luxury of observing in peace from afar

been talking to Harry
if push came to shove
agreed we could survive out here
self-reliant
all the basics covered
water and food
ammunition even

hard to say
how gnarly it may become
terrible to even imagine
this difficult beautiful world
so messed up
messed up by the best brains to ever evolve
so sad possibly

seems to me there are solutions
this our real challenge
how we treat the planet
so often still speak of nature as if another thing
yet we are nature
just one more living thing
knowing so much life already extinct at our own hand

the planet
of course
will be fine
even flourish in many ways
without us
surely though
this need not be

solutions surely anchored in us
how we treat each other
how we interact
listen
honour our past mistakes
envision a future equitably
action one hope at a time

some out here call me idealistic
aiming unrealistically high
my own dad recently included
guilty as charged I say
happily guilty of that
what's the alternative eh
lower my sights I suppose

throw my hands in the air
give up
despair
aim for mediocrity
see no joy there
have to aim high
if we don't get there at least we tried

what's that saying
would rather die on my feet
than live on my knees
we're at that point I reckon
a fight on our hands
but it has to be a fight together
if not we really are stuffed

a beautiful night here
another calm lovely cool night
hard to imagine anything wrong anywhere
no sickness from here can I see
no streets full of conflict surround me
perhaps I should just hunker down
thank my lucky stars as I watch another clear moon rise

when you gaze at the moon
from wherever you are
I too am staring at the same
the same sphere
reflecting light
back on us both
same rabbit up there frozen in time

unchanged since Caesar gazed
perhaps prayed to it
before battle or lavish meal
Buddha too and that Plato there
Mohammad and Jesus
all at some time
gazed with wonder upon the same

a sailer today
or one in ancient times
beneath rough simple sails
appreciated its various light and tides
both relying on the same arc
a constant above
amid seas of change

the moon unchanged
yet the tides are not the same
swells reach higher
thanks to our greed and stupidity
what would Buddha think now
knowing changes unfurled by man
climate shifting but our behaviour unmoved

white and male
living in Australia
totally free
could do anything me
such luck
layer upon layer
how much am I really doing

love your Buddha quote
before enlightenment
chop wood
carry water
after enlightenment
chop wood
carry water

I could work all day
create something
fix something
or I could go to the pub
do nothing
achieve nothing
only one of these would make me sad

that grog
I am so ashamed
all the choices
mostly bad
drinking
even the choice to drink at all
such wasted time

plus of course
your opinion perhaps of me
consequently
sorry am I
yet what can you do
undoing the past
a little complex

only thing I guess
and I thank Arthur's example for this
is to admit all
offer apologies
to others
and to the finer version of self
a self that may have been if not for grog

then move forward
embracing every clear eyed morning
sad such logic didn't come before
but grateful it came at all
and meeting you of course
a part of this
wanting more than anything to please

gain approval
lots to ponder
on this old veranda
so far from you
so much to do
always missing you
Callum

Dear Hiroyuki
thank you so much for your letter
yesterday received
so difficult no doubt
for you to write
and me to read
such sadness suddenly

cannot believe she is gone
this illness you say
this virus dreaded everywhere
I had begun to wonder if all was OK
two letters unanswered worried me
just in her last mentioned feeling unwell
now I have nothing to hold but my tears

Yukie's ashes to Kirinya
her wish you say
when flights possible again
borders open
though never the same world
such hope I had
all gone

yesterday
read your letter
your heavy news
read it again and again
spoke to Harry
read it again
hoping for anything but the same news

Harry's over at Broken Hill
would have been good to spend time with him
so decided to walk
stride out
stretch out
think some things through
view my world through teary different eyes

walked down and along the river
seemed that every tree
every saltbush scrub
looked different to before
sat on the same big old redgum log
long dead hanging up high on the levee exposed
a photo I took there of you and she

hate to say it
but I rolled a cigarette down there
then another
sucked it in deep too
that dreaded nicotine
Yukie would not approve
but it did help me think some more

reckon the pub beckons soon
Mum and Dad are on their way
really upset of course also
suggested we meet at the pub
way too sad for me out here
see her face in every room
hoped it would again be that way

please give your parents my best regards
so sad for you all
such a treasure as she
dear Yukie
shall try to write again in a few days
best regards my friend
Callum

Dear Hiroyuki
these weeks
these few long weeks since your news
nothing makes sense any more
yet I am trying
even if my shoulders feel heavy
these often blue skies here look somehow grey

Harry's been brilliant
such a friend
insisted I stay over there a while
talked so much
sadly he knows grief well
so many has he lost
so many he's had to farewell

we even got to planning again
he had me working of course
every day
can't stop the thinking perhaps
he would say
the sadness don't stop
but you just have to keep moving

I remembered something
once said to Yukie
or perhaps in a letter it was
an old quotation I'd heard
as I recall it
the situation is hopeless
we must take the next step

Harry liked it too
that's it exactly bud
that's life I'm afraid said he
hard as it be
and what you should be doing then
said my huge-hearted friend
you should live every day to make her proud

so
Hiroyuki
that's exactly what I promise you now
I want to honour her memory through my trying
Yukie I am sure
battled until her last breath
tried right until the end

your grandfather and mine
struggled in their own different ways
fought for life in that stupid war
for the next generation
just think of the generations all gone
me here on Paarkintji land
tens of thousands of years people here

hardship and joy
death and new life
my Scottish ancestors
the same but different battles
you in Japan with that fantastic lineage
suffering and beauty
austerity and plenty

my life
on balance
weighed up against the suffering of others
then and now
ridiculous in its ease
an embarrassment of riches
even despite my heartache now

so much for us to do
here and elsewhere
on this patch of the earth
so many challenges everywhere
altogether a mountain unending to climb
so to keep our sanity Harry and I agreed
need to target one peak at a time

but we do need to engage our brains
push back against stupid greed
listen more to each other
and the earth
give more than take
sow more than reap
create more than consume

live each day
better than yesterday
simpler I mean
in a way that Yukie would be proud
our forebears would be proud
so that when rest does come
we can sleep with dignity

we can close our eyes
tired from our honest efforts
with pride not in the completion
for no generation can fix all
but close our eyes calm
at peace with ourselves
our example and our efforts to be

I do get it
I mean I think I see
why some bail out
all becomes too much
clouds just keep rolling in
many a lonely farmer out here
sadly found no other way

your country too
quite a relationship with suicide eh
yet not for me
no matter how sad I may be
Harry across the river
the Paarka trying so hard to flow
so much good there could be

and something Yukie said
something she wrote to me
I want to share with you
hope you don't mind
your sister's lovely words
had no idea at the time
the last she'd send to me

Dear Callum
I am not well
when I close my eyes
finding it difficult to breathe
I have a picture of you
in my weary mind
each time I close my eyes

that day you showed me the tree
the Leopardwood tree
such a beautiful and elegant thing
its bark mottled orange and grey
standing proud on that flat land
that vast ochre land of yours
with your sky so blue

such a lovely pale blue
where on the horizon
so far
the earth's curve may be perceived
and do you remember that day
you picked up a small dead limb
beneath that Leopardwood tree

raised it up to show me
and there hiding
beneath the bark
that small dark gecko of velvet brown
such a sweet little thing
almost lost in your hand
so small and frightened

yet you so gentle
resting it back to the ground
placing its shelter as it was
I so wish it was that day again
but I have the memory
a treasure to me
and I only have it to hold

only have it because we made it
we made the most of that day
and who knows how many we can make
separately or together
until then though and always
my eyes will close
peacefully

an image of you
caring for the little creature
thoughtfully
and with all your wonderful energy
caring for your country
my love
Yukie

www.ingramcontent.com/pod-product-compliance
Lightning Source LLC
Chambersburg PA
CBHW070937080526
44589CB00013B/1542